Numbers

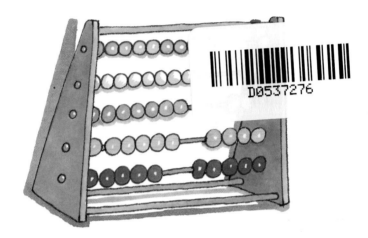

Les nombres

leh *nahm*-br'

Illustrated by Clare Beaton

Illustré par Clare Beaton

b small publishing

one

1 2 3 4 5 6 7 8 9 10

1

un

ahn

two

1 2 3 4 5 6 7 8 9 10

1 2 3 4 5 6 7 8 9 10

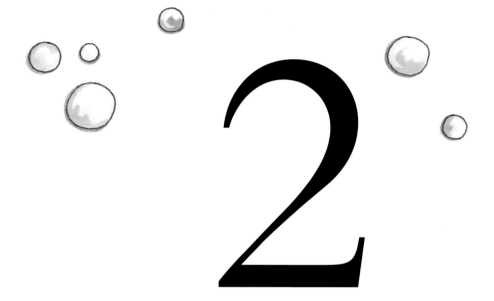

2

deux

three

1 2 3 4 5 6 7 8 9 10

1 2 3 4 5 6 7 8 9 10

3

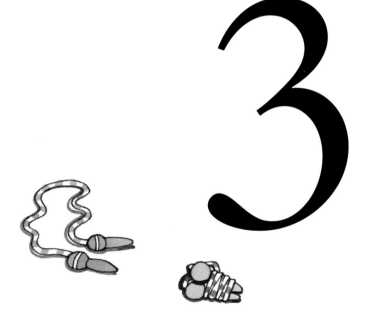

trois

trwah

four

1 2 3 4 5 6 7 8 9 10

1 2 3 4 5 6 7 8 9 10

4

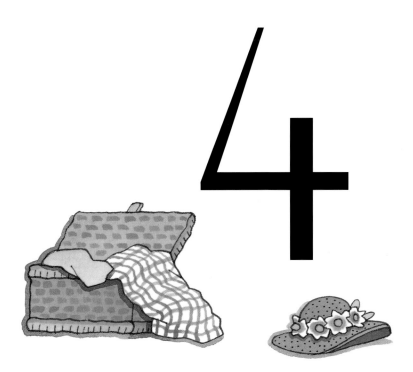

quatre

cat

five

1 2 3 4 **5** 6 7 8 9 10

1 2 3 4 5 6 7 8 9 10

5

cinq

sank

six

1 2 3 4 5 6 7 8 9 10

1 2 3 4 5 6 7 8 9 10

6

six

seven

1 2 3 4 5 6 7 8 9 10

1 2 3 4 5 6 7 8 9 10

7

sept

set

eight

1 2 3 4 5 6 7 8 9 10

1 2 3 4 5 6 7 8 9 10

8

huit

weet

nine

1 2 3 4 5 6 7 8 9 10

1 2 3 4 5 6 7 8 9 10

neuf

nerf

ten

1 2 3 4 5 6 7 8 9 10

1 2 3 4 5 6 7 8 9 10

10

dix

deess

1 2 3 4 5

one   **two**   **three**   **four**   **five**

un   deux   trois   quatre   cinq

6 7 8 9 10

six **seven** **eight** **nine** **ten**

six sept huit neuf dix

A simple guide to pronouncing the French words

- Read this guide as naturally as possible, as if it were standard British English.
- Put stress on the letters in *italics* e.g. leh *nahm*-br'
- Don't roll the r at the end of the word, e.g. in the French word le (the): ler.

Les nombres	leh *nahm*-br'	**Numbers**
un	ahn	**one**
deux	d'	**two**
trois	trwah	**three**
quatre	cat	**four**
cinq	sank	**five**
six	seess	**six**
sept	set	**seven**
huit	weet	**eight**
neuf	nerf	**nine**
dix	deess	**ten**

Published by b small publishing
The Book Shed, 36 Leyborne Park, Kew, Richmond, Surrey, TW9 3HA, UK
www.bsmall.co.uk
© b small publishing, 1993 and 2008 (new cover)
2 3 4 5 6
All rights reserved.
Printed in China by WKT Company Ltd.
ISBN-13: 978-1-874735-00-7 (UK paperback)
Cataloguing-in-Publication Data:
A catalogue record for this book is available from the British Library